Johannes Brahms

Piano Concertos Nos. 1 and 2
in Full Score

From the Breitkopf & Härtel Complete Works Edition

Edited by Hans Gál

DOVER PUBLICATIONS, INC.
Mineola, New York

Bibliographical Note

This Dover edition, first published in 2007, is an unabridged republica-
tion of Volume 6 *(Konzerte für Klavier und Orchester)* of *Johannes Brahms;
Sämtliche Werke; Ausgabe der Gesellschaft der Musikfreunde in Wien*, originally
published by Breitkopf & Härtel, Leipzig, ca. 1926–1927. Editor's
Commentary dated spring 1927. The Editor's Commentary was translated
by Stanley Appelbaum for the present edition.

International Standard Book Number
ISBN 13: 978-0-486-46414-5
ISBN 10: 0-486-46414-8

Manufactured in the United States of America
Dover Publications, Inc., 31 East 2nd Street, Mineola, N.Y. 11501

CONTENTS

EDITOR'S COMMENTARY

PIANO CONCERTO NO. 1 IN D MINOR, OP. 15

SOURCE TEXTS:

1. The score edition of the Verlag Rieter-Biedermann (now C. F. Peters in Leipzig).
2. Brahms's personal working copy of the score, in the possession of the Gesellschaft der Musikfreunde in Vienna.
3. Brahms's personal working copy of the first edition for piano solo (Rieter-Biedermann), in the possession of the Gesellschaft der Musikfreunde in Vienna.
4. The Rieter-Biedermann edition for two pianos.

REMARKS:

The concerto was published in 1861, but only in orchestral parts and for piano solo (source text 3). The score and the two-piano edition did not appear until 1875. A newly engraved score was published by C. F. Peters in 1918. The original title reads: "Concert für das Pianoforte mit Begleitung des Orchesters componiert von Johannes Brahms. Op. 15." Publication number 815.

The score, which, as has been mentioned, was published much later, contains a number of insignificant printing errors. The two editions for piano (source texts 3 and 4) were prepared with unusual care and are virtually free of error, so that in cases of discrepancies they were generally given the preference. These discrepancies follow:

In Movement 1, m. 78, the score gives Clarinet 1 a *c* on the fourth quarter; this has been corrected to *a*.

At the beginning of the piano solo in m. 91, the score lacks the indicated *p espress.* that appears in both piano editions. Similarly, the score lacks the "Poco più moderato" for the second theme of Movement 1 on both occurrences as well as the corresponding restoration of tempo "Tempo I."

In m. 255, the score gives the piano:

In m. 278, the score gives the piano upper staff as:

and, correspondingly, in mm. 281–282:

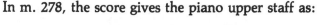

In his personal working copy, Brahms sketched the correction in pencil, and it is already adopted in source texts 3 and 4. In mm. 469–470 the score gives the piano:

A few striking departures from uniformity in details of instrumentation and phrasing in parts of the recapitulation that are otherwise exactly analogous to the exposition (especially noteworthy is the missing woodwind upbeat in m. 399 vis-à-vis the corresponding m. 175!) had to be retained since there is agreement in all source texts.

In Movement 3, m. 20, source text 3 gives the piano *d*-sharp in the upper staff; Brahms crossed out the sharp sign there, and this change was already made in source texts 1 and 4. At the last eighth note in m. 21, and likewise in m. 156, the score gives "poco sosten.," and two mm. later "a tempo." In the piano editions this nuance does not come until the last reappearance of the theme, in m. 309. In m. 232, the score gives the double bass *f* instead of *e*-flat. In m. 463 in the first piano edition the left hand has the octave *D* tied for eight mm. without new attacks. In the personal copy (source text 3) the ties are crossed out every other measure; this change was made in the score, but the ties remain in source text 4.

Numerous small errors in the score, especially missing accidentals, ties and slurs, staccato dots and the like in the piano part, were altered on the basis of source texts 3 and 4. The relative unreliability of the score in comparison to the piano editions is apparently due to the fact that, being published much later, it was not newly compared against the very carefully checked piano edition.

PIANO CONCERTO NO. 2
IN B-FLAT MAJOR, OP. 83

SOURCE TEXTS:
1. The Simrock edition of the score.
2. Brahms's personal working copy of the score, in the possession of the Gesellschaft der Musikfreunde in Vienna.
3. The Simrock "Edition for Piano Solo."
4. The original MS, in the possession of Prof. Robert Freund in Budapest.

REMARKS:
The concerto was published in 1882 by N. Simrock, Berlin, with the title: "Concert (No. 2 B dur) für Pianoforte mit Begleitung des Orchesters von Johannes Brahms. Op. 83." Over this is the dedication: "Seinem theuren Freunde und Lehrer Eduard Marxsen zugeeignet." Publication number 8263.

The score contains a few insignificant engraving errors. One of them is corrected in the personal copy (a missing flat sign in front of the *d* in the double bass, Movement 3, m. 44), which has no other handwritten entry. A mistaken natural sign in front of the *e*-flat in the Violin 1 part in Movement 3, m. 42 (Oboe 1 at the same point has *e*-flat, which also occurs in the piano solo edition) was eliminated. The solo edition includes no differences from the piano part in the score.

The original MS, which was obviously used as engraving copy, has numerous corrections in Brahms's hand, all of which involve details of instrumentation, as well as entries in another hand relative to details of the engraving process. A great number of small tempo changes added in blue pencil (Movement 1, m. 118 "animato," m. 128 "poco sostenuto," m. 286 "sostenuto," m. 291 "in tempo," m. 332 "un poco sostenuto," etc.) were crossed out again later—seemingly to avoid chopping up the tempo, but nevertheless a clear indication that the composer intended a certain freedom in performance. The original tempo indication of the finale was "Allegro non troppo e grazioso."

VIENNA, SPRING 1927   HANS GÁL

REVISIONSBERICHT

KLAVIER-KONZERT Nr. 1 D MOLL. Op. 15

VORLAGEN:

1. Die Partiturausgabe des Verlags Rieter-Biedermann (jetzt C. F. Peters in Leipzig).
2. Brahms' Handexemplar der Partitur, im Besitz der Gesellschaft der Musikfreunde in Wien.
3. Brahms' Handexemplar der ersten Klavierausgabe (Rieter-Biedermann), im Besitz der Gesellschaft der Musikfreunde in Wien.
4. Die Rieter-Biedermannsche Ausgabe für zwei Klaviere.

BEMERKUNGEN:

Das Konzert erschien 1861, jedoch bloß Orchesterstimmen und Klavierausgabe (Vorlage 3). Erst 1875 erschien die Partitur und die Ausgabe für zwei Klaviere. Eine neugestochene Partitur ist 1918 bei C. F. Peters erschienen. Der ursprüngliche Titel lautet: »Concert für das Pianoforte mit Begleitung des Orchesters componiert von Johannes Brahms. Op. 15.« Verlagsnummer 815.

Die, wie erwähnt, viel später erschienene Partitur enthält eine Anzahl unbedeutender Druckfehler. Den beiden Klavierausgaben (Vorlage 3 und 4), die ungemein sorgfältig bezeichnet und so gut wie fehlerlos sind, wurde deshalb, wo Differenzen bestehen, im allgemeinen der Vorzug gegeben. Solche sind nachstehend angeführt:

Im 1. Satz Takt 78 hat in der Partitur die 1. Klarinette auf dem 4. Viertel *c*, das nach *a* richtiggestellt wurde.

Beim Einsatz des Klaviersolos im 91. Takt fehlt in der Partitur die Bezeichnung *p espress.*, die in beiden Klavierausgaben enthalten ist. Ebenso fehlt in der Partitur beim Seitenthema des 1. Satzes beidemal das »*Poco più moderato*« und die entsprechende spätere Wiederherstellung »*Tempo I*«.

Takt 255 lautet in der Partitur das Klavier folgendermaßen:

Takt 278 lautet in der Partitur das obere System des Klaviers folgendermaßen:

und entsprechend Takt 281—282:

Im Handexemplar ist die Korrektur von Brahms mit Bleistift skizziert, die in den Vorlagen 3 und 4 bereits durchgeführt ist. Takt 469—470 lautet das Klavier in der Partitur folgendermaßen:

Einige auffallende Inkonsequenzen in Bezug auf Satz- und Phrasierungseinzelheiten in den der Exposition sonst genau konformen Teilen der Reprise (besonders auffallend der fehlende Holzbläserauftakt im Takt 399 gegenüber dem entsprechenden Takt 175!) mußten, da in allen Vorlagen übereinstimmend, bestehen bleiben.

Im 3. Satz Takt 20 steht in der Vorlage 3 im oberen System des Klaviers ♯ *dis*; das ♯ ist dort von Brahms gestrichen, was in den Vorlagen 1 und 4 bereits durchgeführt ist. Beim letzten Achtel im 21. Takt und ebenso im 156. Takt steht in der Partitur »*poco sosten.*«, zwei Takte später »*a tempo*«. In den Klavierausgaben steht diese Nüance erst bei der letzten Reprise des Themas, im 309. Takt. Im 232. Takt hat in der Partitur der Kontrabaß *f* anstatt *es*. Im 463. Takt hat in der ersten Klavierausgabe die linke Hand durch acht Takte die Oktave D gebunden, ohne Wiederanschlag. Im Handexemplar (Vorlage 3) sind die Bindebogen jeden zweiten Takt gestrichen, welche Änderung in der Partitur durchgeführt ist, wogegen in der Vorlage 4 noch die Bogen stehen.

Zahlreiche kleine Fehler in der Partitur, namentlich fehlende Versetzungszeichen, Bogen, Staccatopunkte u. dgl. im Klavierpart, wurden nach den Vorlagen 3 und 4 richtiggestellt. Die relative Unverläßlichkeit der Partitur im Vergleich zu den Klavierausgaben scheint dadurch erklärt, daß bei ihrem verspäteten Erscheinen offenbar keine neuerliche Vergleichung mit der sehr sorgfältig revidierten und bezeichneten Klavierausgabe vorgenommen wurde.

————

KLAVIER-KONZERT Nr. 2 B DUR. Op. 83

VORLAGEN:

1. Die Simrocksche Druckausgabe der Partitur.
2. Brahms' Handexemplar der Partitur, im Besitz der Gesellschaft der Musikfreunde in Wien.
3. Die Simrocksche »Ausgabe für Pianoforte solo«.
4. Die Originalhandschrift, im Besitz von Prof. Robert Freund in Budapest.

BEMERKUNGEN:

Das Konzert erschien im Jahre 1882 bei N. Simrock in Berlin, mit dem Titel: »Concert (No. 2 B dur) für Pianoforte mit Begleitung des Orchesters von Johannes Brahms. Op. 83«. Darüber die Widmung; »Seinem theuren Freunde und Lehrer Eduard Marxsen zugeeignet.« Verlagsnummer 8263.

Die Partitur enthält wenige unbedeutende Stichfehler. Ein einziger ist im Handexemplar richtiggestellt (ein fehlendes ♭ vor *des* im Kontrabaß, 3. Satz, 44. Takt), das sonst keinerlei Eintragungen enthält. Ein falsches ♮ vor *es* in der 1. Violine im 3. Satz, 42. Takt (in der 1. Oboe steht gleichzeitig *es*, in der Klaviersoloausgabe ebenfalls *es*) wurde beseitigt. Die Soloausgabe zeigt keinerlei Abweichungen von der Klavierstimme der Partitur.

Die Originalhandschrift, die augenscheinlich als Stichvorlage benutzt wurde, zeigt zahlreiche Korrekturen von Brahms' Hand, die durchwegs Details der Instrumentation angehen, sowie stichtechnische Eintragungen von fremder Hand. Eine große Anzahl mit Blaustift hinzugesetzter kleiner Temporückungen (im 1. Satz Takt 118 »animato«, Takt 128 »poco sostenuto«, Takt 286 »sostenuto«, Takt 291 »in tempo«, Takt 332 »un poco sostenuto« u. a.) sind nachträglich wiederum gestrichen; anscheinend, um die Einheitlichkeit der Temponahme nicht zu gefährden, jedoch ein deutlicher Hinweis auf die Absicht einer gewissen Freiheit des Vortrags. Die Tempobezeichnung des Finales war ursprünglich »Allegro non troppo e grazioso«.

Wien, im Frühjahr 1927.

Hans Gál.

Piano Concerto No. 1 in D Minor, Op. 15

Rondo

Piano Concerto No. 2 in B-flat Major, Op. 83

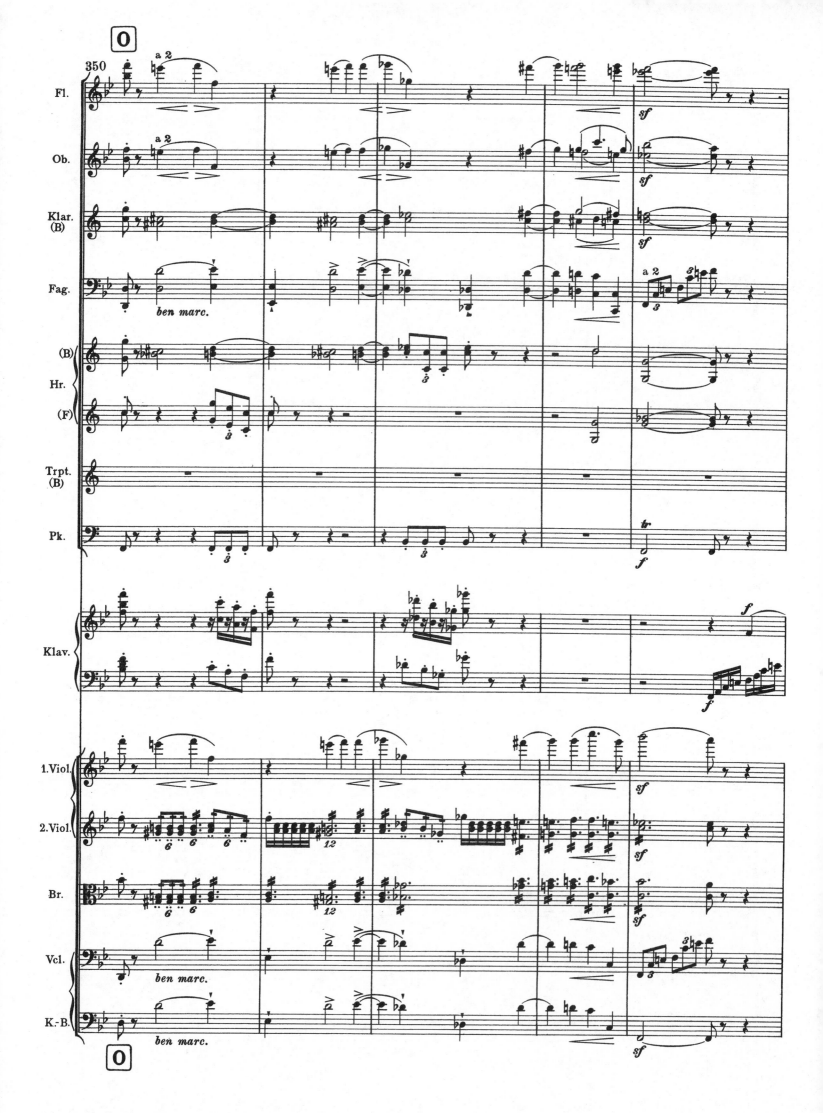